PRAISE FOR

The Relativity of Living Well

"This is not about me," writes Ashna Ali, and "Here. Taste this." I see the poems in *The Relativity of Living Well* as compassionate and fervent calls to arms in a time where so much seems ungrounded and uncertain. Ali reminds us to consider the borders where the individual meets the collective, and where the collective meets the larger global world. It is in those spaces, they suggest, that the radical work of living must occur: through the everyday act of not just breaking bread, but also making it. Reader, I trust you to relish and cherish these tender and precise ruminations as I do.

—Tarfia Faizullah, author of *Seam* and *Registers of Illuminated Villages*

Ashna Ali is Distinguished Professor of Grief in *The Relativity of Living Well*, a short collection that traces the first months of the pandemic in New York City. These poems instructively plunge deep into the consequences and costs of the US-American obsession with productivity.

What's more, Ali teaches the reader to analyze the gestures of our fellow grieving citizenry. "What if not a single medical worker hears the 7pm clamor?" If skeptical, their read is honest to the core. "I have to call things by their names before they ooze back together."

They expose the despair inherent in working through a serious illness in a city hard-struck by not just the virus, but bureaucratic jockeying and governmental gaslighting that prizes optics over human life. It's an important work of documentation, particularly in 2021's rush to get back to normal in the wake of catastrophe--after which, for so many, normal is forever lost.

—Krystal Languell

The Relativity of Living Well cascades of heart sunken and spirit trying! Ashna Ali conjures a spectrum of emotions which poignantly survive the empire. Brimming in reportage, memoir, and exploration, these stanzas harness daily sinew of a landscape in crisis. Ali delivers humor, reflection, pain, and peril with staggering texture. They ask us in the swell of racial injustice, "Have you learned yet? The difference between fireworks and gunshots?" How deliberate, vulnerable, gut wrenching! As a Queer, Muslim, and Bangladeshi educator, Ali has gifted us a nuanced poetry debut —incredible and dismantling.

—Kay Ulanday Barrett, 2021 Barbara Gittings Stonewall Honor Book & 2021 Lambda Literary Finalist Award-winning author of *More Than Organs*

What forms—of work, of love, of living, of language—can and will sustain us? Ashna Ali's diaristic poems, written through the spring and into the summer of 2020, trace both the systemic failures of government responses to the COVID-19 pandemic and the acts of community support and survival that flourished in the face of these failures. These poems find tenderness in "new ways of saying we like each other / alive": a student wiping a teacher's desk with bleach, a lover brewing tea, a Zoom seminar, a demonstration in defense of Black Trans Lives. These survival strategies, Ali reminds us, are beautiful, but are not a distraction from the witnessing and rage this moment calls for. "This is America," they write: "There's no room for grief we can't sell."

—MC Hyland

The Relativity of Living Well

The Relativity of Living Well

ASHNA ALI

the operating system c. 2021

```
the operating system
kin(d)* / in corpore sano
autonomous mechanics print//document
```

The Relativity of Living Well

ISBN: 978-1-946031-97-6
Copyright © 2022 by Ashna Ali
Editing, cover design and typography by Elæ Moss
Cover and frontispiece illustrations by Deva H. Navarro
Interior design by Natalie C. Sousa and Elæ Moss, using the OS Open Access Design Protocol

is released under a Creative Commons CC-BY-NC-ND (Attribution, Non Commercial, No Derivatives) License: its reproduction is encouraged for those who otherwise could not afford its purchase in the case of academic, personal, and other creative usage from which no profit will accrue.
Complete rules and restrictions are available at: http://creativecommons.org/licenses/by-nc-nd/3.0/
For additional questions regarding reproduction, quotation, or to request a pdf for review contact **operator@theoperatingsystem.org**

This text was set in Savate, FreightSans Pro, and OCR-A Standard. Our house body font, Freight, was designed by American typeface designer Joshua Darden. Its organic shape and balance make it an approachable and readable typeface. It is part of our continued commitment to supporting often invisible BIPOC type designers. Savate, our title font, is used via a SIL Open Font License, through Velvetyne Type Foundry. It was designed by Wech. All type on VTF is libre and open-source, and fully aligned with the OS's mission.
Support and learn more at https://velvetyne.fr

Books from The Operating System are distributed to the trade via Ingram, with additional production by Spencer Printing, in Honesdale, PA, in the USA. As of 2020 all titles are also available for donation-only download via our Open Access Library: www.theoperatingsystem.org/os-open-access-community-publications-library/

Cover Description: A digital illustration of the author and their friend sitting. at a distance from one another on the same stair of a brownstone stoop, holding coffees. Neither figure has facial features. In the window to the right of the front door, a man is cooking. The image is entirely constructed in shades of blue, gray, black, and white. The title, The Relativity of Living Well, stretches out on the asphalt in white. On the bottom of the guard rails, text in yellow reads, "ashna ali" and "poems' on either side of the entryway.

The Operating System is a member of the Radical Open Access Collective, a community of scholar-led, not-for-profit presses, journals and other open access projects. Now consisting of 40 members, we promote a progressive vision for open publishing in the humanities and social sciences.
Learn more at: http://radicaloa.disruptivemedia.org.uk/about/

Your donation makes our publications, platform and programs possible! We <3 You.
https://www.theoperatingsystem.org/subscribe-join/

```
the operating system
```
www.theoperatingsystem.org
IG: @the_operating_system
tweet tweet : @the_os_

For everyone lost in the fight against COVID-19.
For everyone martyred against their will.
For everyone failed by the U.S. American state.
For everyone harboring wild dreams
of another entirely possible world.

TABLE OF CONTENTS

FOREWORD	1
INFECTION	4
DENIAL	5
ANGER	6
BARGAINING	7
DEPRESSION, DOING DISHES BY THE WINDOW AT BOTH ENDS OF THE DAY	8
DEPRESSION, DOOMSCROLLING	9
ACCEPTANCE: A SURVIVAL GUIDE	10
WHEN THE PLAGUE BRINGS WITH IT DARK DREAMS OF SCAVENGERS	11
THE RELATIVITY OF LIVING WELL	14
I KNOW THAT THE KILLING OF THIS DEVIL IS THE BEGINNING OF BLISS*	15
OBJECT LESSONS IN ONTOLOGY	16
POWER	17
SOCIAL DISTANCE THEORY	18
SELF PORTRAIT IN SUSPENSION	21
OVER COFFEE I WRITE LETTERS TO NEOLIBERAL DEATH CULTS	22
ASSISTED RELEASE	24
PLAGUE SUMMER SOUNDSCAPE	25
TRUMP THREATENS TO DEFUND EDUCATION IF SCHOOLS REFUSE TO OPEN AMIDST GLOBAL PANDEMIC	26
THE BAD PLACE	27
THERE IS STILL NO PUBLIC MOURNING BUT I AM ASKED TO KEEP LEARNING AND BE THANKFUL AND IMPRESSED	28
GRIEF CATALOGUE	29
WE LIVE ON LOVE	31
ACKNOWLEDGEMENTS	33
STILLNESS AND SOLACE / A FIST TO THE STARS: an OS [RE:CON]VERSATION	34
BACKMATTER	38

FOREWORD
heidi andrea restrepo rhodes

Aristotle's notion of "the good life" (Greek: *eudaimonia – eu: good/well; daimon: spirit*)—which is commonly translated as "happiness" or "welfare" but is perhaps better translated as a kind of "human flourishing" or "blessedness"—has long been twisted by western capitalism and coloniality, packaged neatly in the US into "the American Dream" and sold to anyone living within the bounds of this country as an individualist project maximizing consumerism and productivity: a fiction that has peaked in its unsustainability through the many months of the COVID-19 Pandemic. Ashna Ali's collection, *The Relativity of Living Well*, exposes that fiction through lyrical narrative poems that bring into question what the good life actually means in, through, and beyond the space and time of pandemic life, illness, and death. Across these pages, Ali offers us necessary social commentary while storying glimpses of life in New York City lived as a queer, agender, disabled/chronically sick, Desi-Italian immigrant teacher coping, surviving, and loving, in a pandemic unfolding under capitalist mandates and neoliberal austerities (what Ali poignantly calls "death cults"), as well as heightened fascism, public response of protest, and a dysfunctional government failing its people through an extended public health crisis.

I write this foreword as 2020 comes to an end, a pandemic year in the United States marked by a 30% unemployment rate, heightened psychological and physical stress, ongoing national patterns of anti-black and anti-indigenous police brutality, lynchings, compromised schooling and beyond-exhausted parents, shuttered public life and commerce, isolation born of enforced "social distancing" to stop viral spread, an underfunded healthcare system putting "essential workers" at high risk, over 340,000 deaths nationally (and counting), make-shift morgues and mass graves, and the general depletion of collective spirit and morale. I feel the unbearable weight of our times carried across these poems. Not to mention the further-reaching impact beyond US American borders: these poems also remove us from the solipsisms of US media to linger in the international terrains of racism's effects, anti-Chinese, anti-Muslim, anti-black, and anti-refugee sentiments conflating modernity's "others" with contagion (see, for example, "Depression, Doomscrolling"; and "When the Plague Brings with it Dark Dreams of Scavengers"). It has been a year of devastations. There is so much to grieve, but, as Ali reminds us:

> *this is America. There's no room for grief we can't sell.*

Here, in these pages, Ali's writing is gut-punch and grief, survival and brilliance, critical in its thought and beautiful in its language without commodifying or romanticizing this disaster we've been living; insisting that mourning have place in the everyday living under empire. Threaded through with Kübler-Ross' five stages of grief stacked up in the wake of the pandemic's traumas, *The Relativity of Living Well* begins with infection, (notably, Ali's own), and takes us through denial, anger, bargaining, depression, and acceptance. But not acceptance as resignation. Rather, it is acceptance as public acknowledgement of the great storm we are facing. History's layers of violence seep through the palimpsest of the pandemic present and its racial, classed, and heteropatriarchal inequities. In the face of state denial, negligence, and abandonment, the struggle to survive is also a battle over collective memory when, in "Anger", Ali writes:

> *But face it: we know*
>
> *exactly which gods are hanging by the ankle.*
>
> *Whose hands are wrapped around their bones.*
>
> *Which books they'll burn when we're gone.*

It is an ethic of a subaltern remembrance, memory of the subjugated, that underlies this collection's substance as a form of social documentation of the erasures enacted by the state, right-wing culture, and its media hounds, and bearing witness to this era's suspension of life that has brought our very understandings of self-hood and relation into question. In "Self Portrait in Suspension," Ali transforms the poem itself into a selfie and interrogates social media as the platform for selfhood and relation—*the new interpersonal*—exposing the absurdity of an alienated everyday in which our virtual existence has come to replace our haptic practices of being together, which has been at the root of so much psychological distress though this time.

Still, this collection clings to *old abilities to make joys from the disparate and forgotten*, scattered with the small delights and sensory pleasures to be found amidst the horrors: rivers and trees, inquisitive and caring students, the company of cats, love letters and harmonies, flower pots, text messages and poetry readings, cars blasting a good beat, orgasms and baked bread, found intimacies that remind us we are still feeling bodies in rhythm with others (*"I feel you I feel you I feel you I feel you."*)

In spite of it all, it ends with love. The good life, or living well—our very, very human flourishing—however relative, is, as so many of us have known, something we ultimately define and cobble together, with others, through ongoing structures of violence and across distances large and small, in those old abilities to make joys. "We live on love," *even when scorched and delirious,* love is the medicine.
        Love is the bond.
        Love is the living.

                              heidi andrea restrepo rhodes
                              December 31, 2020

INFECTION

*The first case of novel coronavirus in New York City was confirmed on
March 1, 2020. Mayor Bill de Blasio kept schools open through March 14, 2020. By May
2020, seventy Department of Education employees died
from COVID-19. More followed.*

On the subway, a midtown suit wears a gas mask,
bare hands protruding from cuffs.

Scrounged surgical masks stretch across faces
smudged with eyeliner, raw, nightmared. Unprotected,

I move hair from my bare face with bare hands. Freeze.
Trap my breath. Turn my music all the way up.

The lopsided desk at the front of my classroom
has been, for the first time, power washed of coffee stains,

corn syrup, unidentified goo. My students sniff bleach trails
on still, old air. Hold their notebooks in their laps.

My favorite rubs my desk down with Clorox.
Just in case, she says. New ways of saying we like each other

alive. I hold a thermos and a white board marker,
gesture as I move my mouth. The motions.

I ask a question. They watch me touch the table, a chair,
the whiteboard. No one raises their hand.

DENIAL

If I hit the self-mute button, my wheezing
is muffled even to me. The neighbor waves
in the window, watches me cough into my fist.
I'm fine, I mime, and bow my head to where the screen
cannot see me. I was always a sickly child,
and anyway, 'tis the season. My mouth fills
with bloodmetal. Was sweat always so cold?
Did late winter always sour my calves?
No aroma or flavor rises, only temperature.
But illness can look different as we age.
Send us craving ice cream cold, make us hot
for coffee, a side of clementine rind on the tongue
for a bit of feeling. The doctor says,
*you are an ideal vessel. It prefers those
it can depend on, communicate through,
frigates to help proselytize elsewhere.
You know this*, he says, *didn't you
spend years studying colonialism?*

ANGER

With each higher death toll, laughter

unlatches my jaw and shakes my skull

until my sound is ancient motherwound.

The sound the gut makes at the last sight

of the moon while dragged by the hair

into a cave. Inhaling flat ash. What they mean

by living history. This is not the first rage

to bray itself from my mouth and never stop.

I'd say, to this future, *I'm sorry*. I'd say,

if only we knew. But face it: we know

exactly which gods are hanging by the ankle.

Whose hands are wrapped around their bones.

Which books they'll burn when we're gone.

BARGAINING

A thermometer hangs from my lips, an irreverent tongue.
On the news, nurses urge people not to shoot.
They say there are no more beds for the wounded.
In the land of bodies plenty we slide into glut,
run out of room for new refuse. This is not about me.

I pad from room to room in flame-retardant pajamas.
Balloon print meant to inspire dreams. American solutions.
I remember this taste: As a child I'd wander the house
sucking on Duracell batteries. Lightbulbs made a habit
of unscrewing themselves and crashing
as close to me as they could fall.

They always missed. *I am young*, I say, *lucky*.
I hang my head, measure my productivity
at the end of each day, pay taxes used to hold
my friends at gunpoint, keep quiet when I can.
Compliant behavior. A show of blood
so it might skip my house.

But even I know that in this country,
what does not catch first fire
just burns more slowly.
That nothing
gets left behind.

DEPRESSION, DOING DISHES BY THE WINDOW AT BOTH ENDS OF THE DAY

A pale egg yolk hovers behind new condos,

its face too grainy to run, too grainy to brushstroke its light

over the water. It sings high songs, trembling a hymn

to sear marrow. Even the reptile puppeteers know

the animal art of sky reading. We know this because

the Empire State Building is set to beat its pointed Empire heart

cherry red after dark. Glug Glug. Unclear what it beats for.

Declaration. Pride. Mercy. Who exactly it tells us

is still breathing.

DEPRESSION, DOOMSCROLLING

Markets fall as New York moves into second month of social distancing. Prime Minister Sheikh Hasina has encouraged all to celebrate Pohela Boishakh digitally in Bangladesh, one of the most populous countries in the world. (My cousins throw parties anyway.) Organized by a young cellist in Japan, high school students perform on Zoom. Italians cautiously relax quarantine rules for book and stationary stores. ("Because nobody goes there," says my father, switching to e-books.) Officials who oversee city-run hospitals are now demanding a doctor's note from any medical staffer who calls in sick. (A woman holds a sign: *I am not a hero. I am being martyred against my will.*) Expert Tips for Video Sex With a Partner or an Audience. Bolsonaro Hits the Streets in Latest Social Distancing Snub. In America, *I ain't afraid, I got the blood of Christ on me!* There are "100 to 200 people per day" dying at home left out of the death toll. Evangelical pastors call it a "phantom plague" produced by the Chinese, label public health workers "pansies." Black and Latino populations are disproportionately affected with largest percentage of deaths among African Americans. (We say, *Our entire conversation around this virus is stained with economic elitism.* And nothing happens.) Dalgona Coffee Goes Viral. New York Officials Caused More Deaths To Maintain "the illusion of education." (We are still trying.) COVID-19 could permanently hurt abortion access nationwide. In India, officials are blaming Muslims for spreading the virus. Rikers Island announces reduced mental health support just as inmate gouges out his left eye as horrified correction officers subdue him with pepper spray. How Queer People Are Getting Off While Staying In. (Some of us aren't.) Garbage pickups tell a tale of two cities, with part of Manhattan shrinking. Sourdough starters are like Tamagotchis for your 30's. Queer Quarantine Bingo. NYC forbids Zoom use for remote learning due to security concerns. Leaders extremely concerned about economic fallout.

ACCEPTANCE: A SURVIVAL GUIDE

let a book hat your head.
cup a mug over your mouth

to predict the weather. check your dark
reflection in the television. flirt!

sit inside a castle fort of whiskey bottles
& squeeze the songs
from your cat's belly.

harmonize.

cut the mundane day with a child
screaming your name.

suspend your body over a city in flames.
record its sound.

play it to your lover
after they dream the apocalypse.

attend every meeting in the nude.
invite the cicadas in. dance!

sign your emails
"I secretly love you."

tell your elders all of your sorrows
using only animal sounds.

mail jackhammer beats to an old flame
as a portrait of your heart.

pray.

WHEN THE PLAGUE BRINGS WITH IT DARK DREAMS OF SCAVENGERS

In April 2020, Italy was one of the countries hardest hit by COVID-19. Its ports were deemed unsafe, so the few remaining search-and-rescue missions that assisted migrants seeking rescue from North African and Middle Eastern civil war, poverty, and climate catastrophe were forced to stop going out onto the Mediterranean Sea. Only one search-and-rescue vessel, the German Alan Kurdi, named after a Syrian toddler whose body was found on the shore in Turkey, was operating.

i.

In the news, the same photos that told what *is* now tell of what *isn't*.
As if the boats ever stopped   pushing off
into promises of diesel leak. The tiltbobweave through gray water
is missing from the pictures. A man who lived to watch says,
After August the good people stop coming so much. The journalists.
In autumn, there's no startling blue for underdogs
in orange to high contrast in hope of rescue.
But under July sun, what a pretty profile
impending death can cut. Even better than drowning.

A headline reads: *I don't know of any law that says if you have
a pandemic you're allowed to let people die in the sea.*
As if all a law must do for dry foot to dry land, for move
from unspeakable places to waiting places, is exist.
As if all a law must do is say so. What would a law know
about what it takes. About what to pick up and what to shed,
how to keep up the project of living. A pregnant woman
offers her calculation for how to decide when her
blooddirtsweat money changes hands: *Even for a pauper's grave
you need willing white people. Masked. Gloved.
Armored in white suits to protect themselves
from you,* but who will haul you up, cut the living
from inside you, name your child, identify your dead.

ii.

A Canadian scientist dropped three carcasses in a body of saltwater
near Vancouver Island, British Columbia. Note the difference:
bodycarcasscorpse. What gets to be a body. What gets to be
a useful remainder. What we deem worthy to bear the promise
of grieving. *Pigs*, the scientist says, *are the best model for humans.*
Roughly the same size, same gut bacteria, relatively hairless.

People of the Book have their reservations.
Pigs have split hooves, but do not chew their cud.
Unclean. Firefighters also abstain from their meat.
They say it smells like human flesh on fire.
Lessons in what kind of uncleanliness
bears too unbearably the stink of kin.

iii.

Unlike the gut flora of the human and the pig,
great white sharks feed happily on the unclean.
For the avian and toothless, the more time spent
floating on the water, the softer the flesh, the more give
to the talon and beak. Supper bruised open by the afternoon sun
until water replaces air in the lungs. bodycarcasscorpse.
Larger carrion eventually join food fall for portuguese dogfish,
and blackmouth catfish. Both are sea sharks with a penchant
for what will not float in the darkness. Not all parts of the body
float. Not all parts of the body sink. *Knowing how bodies degrade*
says the scientist, *can help manage the expectations of family members*
family members lost in the sea under a thousand cameras,
family members lost in the sea by every law that already exists
lost by the hundreds of boats that ignored the distress signals
lost in the ongoing blossom of NASA surveillance.

Knowing how bodies degrade can help manage expectations for those whose deaths are pending. Knowing how bodies degrade plagues the nightmares of family members of those about to be lost at sea.

THE RELATIVITY OF LIVING WELL

I choose to not post about my slack arms,
or anything else. My friends equate this
with silence. They tell me that with nowhere
to go, they pleasure themselves day in, day out.
A camgirl says, *I can't spend all day
dildoing myself!*

I am jealous. Not even the sweet tart
of the season's cherries will do it for me.
Nor the morning birds. I count slowly,
on my fingers: housing, employment,
insurance, limbs, nails, hair, bone.
No dice. So I fill my eyes with whatever
scrolls past, shiny pleasant present-continuous.
I scatter reactions like seeds on concrete:
Heart. Sad face. Heart. Streamers.
Symbols as a marker of space for my body.

A study found that when we wear
headphones and repeat someone else's words,
our navigation skills erode. It's true. We lose how to turn,
when to duck. We walk into walls. I've run out of words
of my own so I parrot in a dread-laced wobble,
hungry for a vestige of oxytocin, evaporating.
Still, I must conjure what hovers when my skin dews
at someone's entrance. Still, I must hope
someone might carve me back
into being.

I KNOW THAT THE KILLING OF THIS DEVIL IS THE BEGINNING OF BLISS*

After Leslie Scalapino

In the beforetime, I'd eat anyone
who someoned the street.
Knives were no strangers,
bliss of beginning, devil this killing know I.

Money needs humans to live.
To order female and male between sex.
To require humans to vote to right
the have-nots under citizens American.
Yet in the morning, coffee thinks me
of killing names, and justice is still hot.

Though the killing of this devil *is* the beginning of bliss,
the name of restraint and the name of civility
curse in the entwining. Meanwhile,
we communicate to language feeling,
to human as someone, dreaming of after,
of when change will language until we meld
into one another's skin without words
to say "I feel you I feel you
I feel you I feel you."

*The title of this poem and several other fragments in it are taken from Leslie Scalapino's "This eating and walking at the same time is associated all right."

OBJECT LESSONS IN ONTOLOGY

A student says, *You can't do that in real life.*
He refers to the act of leaning on a man's neck
with the full weight of one's body for eight minutes
and forty-seven seconds. We consider George Floyd's
real-life dead body and Chauvin's play-pretend badge,
baton, gun. *That's not the real world.*

A student says, *All humans were created equal.*
What happened to the man who can rest his hands
in his pockets while another weeps for his mother?
All creation has a history, I tell them. We talk
about slave patrols, how they grew to become blue
lives, batons, guns, impunity, immunity.

A pass card from being human, says a student.
A uniform that makes you into something else.
We discuss what it means to override human,
crossbreed god and animal. I highlight policy,
but my boys want to talk about another humane:

*What if we could grow up and build a world
without God, but full of sacred?*

POWER

All my friends are pretending not to suffer.
I didn't mean to make this about the police, but what else.
The names of the dead are now too crowded to fit
onto a cardboard sign, front page, or letter.
For every name I memorize are all the names I don't know.
I know that one day a name will belong to our own,
and suddenly, there it is.

A beloved stays up all night posting about a trail of lynching
the media won't cover. Cops take knees and names.
Just this morning I watched guards at Rikers Island laugh
at Layleen Extravaganza Polanco before they let her seize to death.
Only then did a guard become ill herself, retching,
bent over, death rendered real even in the bowels of Hell.
Did Layleen soldier a hard face or did she say hi, hello,
I am human. Where Layleen Extravaganza Polanco lay,
did they allow her to collage the walls with her people
like we do bathroom doors at every queer bar so that
our archives watch as we care for our sinews' mundane magic,
parts that pump hard, precarious, that so often fail without love?

A death of despair is death from a world too long unbearable.
We keep dying, but not dying out. I am supposed to celebrate
because Pride was a riot, but my mouth has never been good
at holding sour with sweet. Just this morning I stood
with fifteen thousand people in front of the Brooklyn Museum
for Black Trans Lives, and then went back to work with voices
shouting "Power!" ringing a bell in my brain. Am not I allowed
to cry no matter how closely the lives we live rub together,
no matter how obvious that we are only just alive?
Have you learned yet? The difference
between fireworks and gunshots?

SOCIAL DISTANCE THEORY

On an assemblage of screens on another firework evening
Ruthie Gilmore reminds us that abolition is not recitation.

Abolition is not recitation of catastrophe. Abolition is not recitation
of catastrophe or culture of complaint. She describes the day;

organized abandonment as condition of neoliberal austerity.
Organized abandonment as made manifest in organized violence.

We gather around the Zoom room to discuss. Remind ourselves
to be reminded of the organization of the familiar familial.

Remind ourselves to be reminded of subtexts of care that feed
on the fiction of scarcity. The closed circuit that makes of itself

protection, the conditions for micro contracts to be kept.
We gather around the Zoom room to discuss.

We discuss living the thinking as the only cure
for failure of the imagination. This looks something like not

being afraid. There are sirens in the back
of more than three unmuted microphones.

Someone asks who has felt cared for lately,
and no one raises their tiny digital hand.

Everyone can find the moment. The total loss of belief
in one's own real, a frequent symptom of the first break

into traumatic normal. It is not only the diseased
national collective but the connection

between loss of real and loss of god
and loss of words. Someone says,

*we are born creative creatures whose first and only
desire is love.* If we were free?

I would not overwork. I would keep more love,
save it up for where it can cast most light rather than burn it out

quickly, leaving me digging at the wick every morning.
I'd tear more open with my teeth. I would keep my knees

slightly bent, ready to slam into anything
that smells good enough to smother with kisses.

I would glisten my pelt with rain
and finger tangle its warmth from sun basking.

I would dig for ancestors. I would swim into low dark
to commune with the eldest lightmakers,

entrust them with my treasures.
In loving and feeling others as I was not,

I can be free and contagious. Together, each time failing again
better, and better, even as they tell us that we do not exist.

Even as they tell us that we are so laughable
that we are deluded. That they're the ones

who know what we really are, who pin price tags
to our skin. I feel proud and strong as much as faint,

skittish. For all this talk, in the pit of the stomach
alongside love sits the naked evidence:

Our destruction does not require imagination.
So many dead, broken, transformed into something

that looks like its master. A tradition.
But we are capable of our own ritual affirmation.

Ruthie reminds us, abolition is presence.
I'm talking about being here in the full flesh

of your body in all of its brokenness
and beautiful mess.

We gather around the Zoom room
to discuss.

SELF PORTRAIT IN SUSPENSION

Art is not documentary. ...its true effort is to open to us dimensions of the spirit of the self that normally lie smothered under the weight of living.
—Jeanette Winterson

Some of my favorite poets come together to read Aracelis Girmay's "You are Who I Love" and I live stream their incantations as the street explodes in pots and pans for the heroes we martyr. May looms. There is no money. I tell my students, *document this moment with the details of your lives*. Winterson asks what lives under the weight of the rise, rinse, commute, labor, repeat. She suggests that images of my face are neither art nor documentation of this living, and yet I check my phone and learn that we do this already as culture and call it power. I am accused of hiding. Instead, what is smothered beneath is that I am dressed like something ceasing to exist. Every day, waking is a canopy of hideous windows creaking open and shut while I lay with eyes as bare as peeled apples. The accidental geometry as they reflect the screen back to itself. The new interpersonal. We are all learning new things. For example, I am apparently a Häagen-Dazs Ruby Cocoa Crackle Pistachio Sweet Cream soul. Who knew. I cannot say this by reversing my camera and pointing from a high angle. But every day, my face babbles questions in the right-hand corner of the Zoom screen. Look at it. What we call a self. As if I have snuck my hand into its hollow to dance its lips, a talking fish. Every live thing has a cycle for its rotting. The day sags with the weight of my hovering for pay. *This* is a selfie. I'm sharing. Look.

OVER COFFEE I WRITE LETTERS TO NEOLIBERAL DEATH CULTS

Gentlemen, I see you.
        today I love that I am   one of your many
  beasties.   big voice. low net worth.
            I see you licking your lips.
    I hear you remind me that my body is for you
to slice open.
    wet fish.
dribble my meager insides out
empty   my pockets of precious.
    remind me
 and remind me   how big you feel
    when I flap
on the pavement   in chorus
    with all the other fish.
    when we pump our gills.   gasp.
        flap.

Gentleman, today I am responsible for the minds   of children.
    today and tomorrow we see you
    anyway.
shift you in your expensive seat redolent   with bleach
    you would shoot
into our veins   if it could make us   dance.
           scale us.
    inhale.   smell me   as I rot   alive.
  watch me
    teach the children words
    how to use them.
show them the incisions.

Gentlemen,
        today I smell as much like you
as like me.
                      mortal.

I see the children   the being of their bodies

      being bodies.

searching their pockets for worth.

        watch me bloat up in the sun.   show them
         how to record.   document.   pile up the evidence.
        even as you eat me and eat me.   round us
        all up by the bank account. so many child beasties
            with their alive bodies thick with words

        and none of the shame in setting you
        on fire.

ASSISTED RELEASE

After months of unfeeling, I reach full body car wreck
by way of empty-bellied white wine in the heat.
My friends hold me up and rearrange me.
They show me evidence of parts in working order.
I wish upon all my loves a plenitude of time.
I think this as I die of my coping mechanisms,
crush the hours in my hands.

Molly says this is our defining trait as a generation,
this looping and losing. I dig through old wounds
in case the backdrops of pandemic and surveillance
tweak the narrative. Negative. Just faster,
more, lots of static, and very very loud. So loud
that the body slips from the present into wound
like a fileted fish into poach water. A small splash
and I am very young, unable to stop anyone
from hooking into my gut for profit,
or power, or play.

Rosann nods her knowing and paints
another flowerpot to show me, as a gift.
Someone texts me to say they're lonely,
they miss everyone, and don't want to talk.
I look for new sentences for love. I pray
for faithful punctuation. heidi teaches me
that form is not everything, but I worry
about outlines, the need to have something
that contains what I cannot hold.

PLAGUE SUMMER SOUNDSCAPE

Shoutout to the partygirl blasting car window summer bops.
Yes, yes, remind me of the shoulderbounce sunkiss of yestersummer.
Remind me how we rolled up to body with one another, winked,
shimmied, all heat & no promises. Now, the songs cut into the chest,
harmonize with the warbling of vans frozen & filling with corpses.
Now, it's a DJ set for a window-attendance-only community funeral.
Now, we bop between two different sirens & know the difference every time.
Today, the radio tells me, a 67-year-old black woman was violently arrested
for writing in pink chalk the words Trump = Plague. Today, the voices
of the young rise together around the block, followed by seven police vans
to pack them into, still alive. I see cops from my window
giving barelegged white boys masks in the park, & calling them sir.
A Talib Kweli throwback reiterates facts into the morning.
This is a kind of quiet. I wanna hear what this new death is,
and I want this quiet to show me. But some kid still pop-pop-pops
cheap fireworks while the clock ticks itself hysterical.
The sound smears itself into familiar fearhush. Wet.
Tendrils in a cowlick of breeze, the sound of ice skaters
lapping a perimeter. Vibration. Soft enough for all the names
to spill their limbs into the frame. Universal inhalation.
The valences of being able to breathe flowering into series.
An aggregation of flexible vectors theorized as hope.
For example, I hear that if I hold this sound for you,
and share it, even that stillness becomes resistant act.
What if not a single medical worker hears the 7pm clamor?
What if the big reveal is, it's really for us? Our labor or our lives.
Keep going, these bells are for you!   Forgive me.
I have to call things by their names before they ooze back together.
Before the whole of my skin beetles itself against the day.
While I butter my bread, the nice lady on the radio
is still talking more sense than we're living.
I want to tell her how slack my food sits in my mouth
while she talks. I want to tell her how loud when I finally swallow.

TRUMP THREATENS TO DEFUND EDUCATION IF SCHOOLS REFUSE TO OPEN AMIDST GLOBAL PANDEMIC

for four months they place our bodies
in shells and fail to notice as we pick
at the stitching. discover the flesh.
capillary root network. soil reverb.

we have begun to talk amongst ourselves.
track body time. the sun rises even when
we do not pay to rent our limbs from ourselves.
yet, even all alone this exhale smacks of stealing.

this country where they sell us our own skin,
place us in the window for children
wearing comparable faces, ask us
to teach them to serve themselves up,
quietly. in a deep spoon. palliative.

this country that taught our fathers
to hold their heads low as survival wisdom.
this country where our mothers
play so much pretend that they knead
truths and lies into the same daily bread
we still eat to live. the swallowing
that makes us of this place.

what if we concoct of this flesh some new medicine.
what if when they wrench us back, new beasts
made from nerve endings, skin turned inside out,
we magic the spoons to hold gasoline, matches,
fire. make new bread of these bodies,
feed the children so that their skin
tells no lies.

THE BAD PLACE

Every gender outlaw in the New York vegetable scene works in the apple section of Fort Greene market, and of course, most of the nose-ringed and ringletted heads overseeing the arsenals of red are white. I sneer at the cottagecore on IG, drop another fifty bucks on bad takeout, and entertain whether a girl named Sunbeam may bring me a sprig of salvation if I could hobby with soil in my fingernails. Instead, I put on a mask once a week and purchase more slave plants gently misted under jaundice lights at the big box store. My lover considers taking another lover who cannot work because they chased a fly who persisted too much, and broke their toe. This the week RBG died.

An old friend made gold by the many times we ripped out the other's gut tells me the next thing is aliens, and I laugh, and he says *no, Ashna, the feds found something made, but not by us, and this is fact—like not fake-fact but fact-fact, The New York Times said.* I cannot !!! that aliens exist. I cannot poke holes in the empire trash rag. I cannot ask about the made-thing-not-by-us. I just slouch, and eat a grape, and say *no. Nope. This is the line,* and draw a squiggle in the air with my foot. And he says, *you know this is the bad timeline where we are our worst selves, and there's another dimension. This is my theory but not really theory, belief.*

What can I do? I raise my glass to the other me out there, thriving, fully realized, prolific, amiable, and brimming with well regulated emotions. The next day, when I count my privileges and stick my head in the fridge for something to do, I am grateful. Grateful for genetically modified baby tomatoes and a half-full bottle of rotgut wine. Grateful that this other Ashna exists. And grateful that I would hate them.

THERE IS STILL NO PUBLIC MOURNING BUT I AM ASKED TO KEEP LEARNING AND BE THANKFUL AND IMPRESSED

Today I am thankful for being a kitchen kid.
Old abilities to make joys from the disparate and forgotten.

Today I learn that my father thought I had a beautiful singing voice
as a child. I want to tell my lover, but I have sent them

to seek peace amongst trees and rivers
so that, upon return, I can melt freshly

on their knees. Again, NYPD copters julienne the sky.
Inspire first fantasies of bazookas.

I learn that a daughter withstands her father's wrath
to hold him through grief like a mother.

I want to tell him that I have mourned a child, but never
learned the word for penis in my mother tongue.

Today, I learn that children know what grown-ups will not say.
That they know themselves as experiment.

My brother teaches me the rules of credit. I learn
how growing up is hooking the stock market to your veins,

and I am certainly a kind of impressed. Italians sang songs
to one another from balconies in lockdown.

But this is America. There's no room for grief we can't sell.

GRIEF CATALOGUE
After Aria Aber

After, we say.
But there is no 'after' for months. There still isn't.
'Cosmic,' as a dimension, establishes itself in the lexicon
        as if we have all always lived with God.
Disallowed despondency dresses as qualified time: a tough day, a long year.
Etymology of grief: Old French from *grever*, a verb. Afflict, burden, oppress.
        A word that describes something done to another, but the subject of the
        sentence somehow always disappears, leaving only the aggrieved. Evaporated
        action.
Futurity recircuits as concept through welcome meme honesty.
Grief, too, is an ecology.
How damage daisy-chains itself across the day.
If feeling particularly florid, or safe, I may sweep the air with a hand
        to mean: survey the obvious. Everyone always nods, but we do not say the
        words regardless.
Jurisdiction tapped back and forth between men huffing and puffing until futility recruits
        as lifestyle through unwelcome meme reality. Inspires
Kalashnikov aspirations. Sometimes.
Love remembers me, sometimes, too. At moments.
Muted mic, dark camera. If no one is there to witness productivity, do we still
        make a sound?
Needlessness is the heart of devouring, I learn. Time's slow rendering into artificial fat.
Ontological oblivions. My face grows into
Palimpsest, cruel optimisms peeking beneath undoing's new shape.
Quoras with strangers for something like remembrance or strategy or solidarity or
Resistance. Even when, still,
Swindle and assessment refuse acknowledgement of one another as kin. Bottom lines.
Talismans made from word fragments left in the chat box from someone with whom
        I cannot meet eyes.
Under. Under the guise of normalcy. Under the boot of. Under the thumb of.
        Underpaid. Undervalued. Underling. Under-stood. Underground. Underway.

Virulent vex voracious in vortex vascular, all over my body, all over my body,
        all over my body. A language, now.
Wanderlust, remember? Ambition. The sky as boundless metaphor. Instead,
Xeroses as possible symptom. Nausea, possible symptom. Insomnia. Migraine.
        Limb-wide ache as web that teaches the skin:
Yes, indeed, you are all a single organ stretched so thin, and you have no choice
        but to feel.

WE LIVE ON LOVE
After Ilya Kaminksy

We live on love
even when scorched and delirious,
nights garbled with sweat. We brew each other's tea,
muster the strength to stand just long enough
to make soup. It passes. We swaddle our hands
in surgical gloves, clothe our faces in masks
just to weigh parmesan in our palms at the grocery store,
giddy with fresh prosciutto and lemon balm,
even if the bread is all gone.

While everyone writes of the slow death
of not being touched, I chop herbs while you
pick playlists to be fed to. Here. Taste this. Mmmm.
While everyone counts the days since they last
touched flesh, I am slathered in kisses. Pinches.
Praise. I regress until all I have to do is lift my chin
to announce my pucker. I always get exactly
what I want. We tent our heads and sip wine
on our stoop, listen to the saxophonist playing
into the mauve sweep of evening, alone.

Everyone sickens, thinks about death.
We stack our mortality against youth,
debate the mystery of what lurks
in our lungs. Even then I tell you the truth:
everything else was always a hindrance
to this living, this food, this living.

ACKNOWLEDGEMENTS

My deepest gratitude to the poets who offered their encouragement, guidance, instruction, and care toward this project (whether or not they knew it), and to the beloveds with whom I share the gift of co-creating joy and survival through this period of pandemic life:

The poem "Trump Threatens to Defund Education If Schools Refuse To Reopen Amidst Global Pandemic" was published in Falsework, Smalltalk: Political Education, Aesthetic Archives, Recitations of a Future in Common, Common Tern Works, Some Beloved, Inc., curated by the Hic Rosa Collective, edited by Asma Abbas and Colin Eubank, 2020

Rafael Varela (always and forever), heidi andrea restrepo rhodes (my dear poetry dom), Elae, Leigh Sugar, Kay Ulanday Barrett, MC Hyland, Henry Mills, Adeeb Ali, Nashwa Zaman, Alexander Arnold, Liza Shapiro, Christopher Perry Wolf, Nicholas Tong, Chelsea Largent, Molly Pearl, Rosann Mariampuram, Peter Torre, Jordan Teicher, Shimrit Lee, Jon Wetter, Deva H. Navarro, Natalie C. Sousa, Alexis Lambrou, Joe Geinart, Dipesh Sinha, Myda El-Maghrabi, Meghan Lastra, Anna Gurton-Wachter, Shira Erlichman, Tarfia Faizullah, Krystal Languell, Yanyi, Emily Brandt, Laura Henriksen, Liz Bowen, Daisy Atterbury, Sara Deniz Akant, and ray ferreira.

STILLNESS AND SOLACE / A FIST TO THE STARS
an OS [RE:CON]VERSATION with ASHNA ALI

Greetings comrade! Thank you for talking to us about your process today! Can you introduce yourself, in a way that you would choose?

I'm Ashna Ali, I'm a queer agender Bangladeshi diasporic poet, writer, researcher, and educator based in Brooklyn.

Why are you a poet/writer/artist?

I have been compelled to express myself in writing ever since I was a child, and over time needed to write, paint, sing, or perform both to connect with others and to feel alive. Ultimately, aren't those the two things we're all stranded on this planet for?

What's a "poet" (or "writer" or "artist") anyway?

To me an artist of any kind is someone who has understood that part of their purpose in the world is to create for themselves and for others, and those those creations have a particular sanctity to them that allows one's spirit to reach those who open themselves to it.

What do you see as your cultural and social role (in the literary/ artistic/ creative community and beyond)?

Perhaps has a result of being an educator of young people, I always think of my role as one of service. I would like my art, my labor, and my actions to serve in the uplift and betterment of the communities of which I am a part, and hopefully offer something to people who could use anything I've learned to feel less alone or more empowered in their own lives.

Talk about the process or instinct to move these poems (or your work in general) as independent entities into a body of work. How and why did this happen? Have you had this intention for a while? What encouraged and/or confounded this (or a chapbook, in general) coming together? Was it a struggle?

Being stranded in my home and deeply ill for several months through 2020 was such a traumatic experience, and the only way I knew to get through it was to write. I documented in journals and I documented in poems, but not with any original intention to string them together into a book object. Eventually, I began to feel the itch to *do something* about the harrowing circumstances around me, but found that lack of time and energy while working full time while sick prevented me from properly participating in mutual aid efforts. Then I thought: "Wait, I have all these poems." I had just been talking to my brilliant bookmaker and poet friend MC Hyland about making books by hand and to OS Founder / Creative director Elæ Moss, in a Liminal Lab workshop about demolishing the fatalism that keeps people from putting work together as final product. I derived a lot of energy and inspiration from both of those conversations and began the process of putting these poems together as poetic memoir to offer as a fundraising object for mutual aid.

I learned how to format poems on word processing documents to print properly on my home laser printer. My dear artist friend Deva H. Navarro kindly drew me an incredible cover image, and I cut and pasted it by hand onto color card to make covers before hand stitching them. I offered them to people in exchange for $5 or more donated to BedStuy Strong, a mutual aid organization that has been working tirelessly to provide resources to the most affected people in my neighborhood and community. People were incredibly generous, and the chapbooks raised over $2000 over the course of a few months.

Elæ then approached me about typesetting the work and publishing it through the OS's Autonomous Documents initiative. I attended several Zoom workshops with Liminal Lab and MC Hyland's Book Making workshop at Center for Book Arts to learn how to make the object more formally and make it available without having to make each copy by hand. I started learning how to use InDesign for the first time and learned a tremendous amount about graphic design, typesetting, fonts, etc. Eventually, I grew sicker and more burnt out from work. I was also doing all of this work on an 11" Macbook Air, which is a very small device to work on for a visual project. I approached my dear friend and talented book designer Natalie Sousa, who has the expertise, experience, devices, and software necessary to develop the project, and she helped me bring this chapbook near completion before handing it off to Elæ for final edits, cover typography and design tweaks.

Did you envision this collection as a collection or understand your process as writing or making specifically around a theme while the poems themselves were being written/the work was being made? How or how not?

Writing poems gave me stillness and solace during a period when I had little hope and little energy. I did not intentially write a poetic memoir, but it was difficult to write about anything but the experience of pandemic life given how all-encompassing and consuming it was. I also wrote other poems on other subjects at the time, but curated these specifically for this project because they happen to be chronological and rather faithful to the arc of experience—mine and seemingly that of many others—during that time. As we continue to live pandemic life (despite so much political pressure to think otherwise), I still struggle to write about other things or not include the details that situate us accordingly.

What formal structures or other constrictive practices (if any) do you use in the creation of your work? Have certain teachers or instructive environments, or readings/ wriitngs/ work of other creative people informed the way you work/ write?

The work included in this particular chapbook often found its seed in prompts received in several workshops I took online in 2020, including In Surreal Life April 2020 with Shira Erlichman and the Writing in Manifold Series curated for the Poetry Project by Sara Jane Stoner. I was also inspired by Cathy Park Hong's speaking and writing on the notion of documentary poetics and her thinking about poets like Solmaj Sharif, Carolyn Forché, Tarfia Faizullah, and Vanessa Angélica Villareal.

Speaking of monikers, how does your process of naming (individual pieces, sections, etc) influence you and/or color your work specifically, beyond this text?

I have a lot of fun with naming individual poems, and I'm a sucker for a good title in everything I read. I tend to pluck phrases from conversation and write them down to steal as titles and create poems around those titles, but occasionally I struggle and have to think seriously about how to give something a name. In short, titles are important to me.

What does this particular work represent to you as indicative of your method/ creative practice?

This chapbook sensitized me to my own interest and curiosity in the notion of the poetic memoir, and how poetry and poetics can be thought of as documentary and archival practice. It's a thread in my thinking and making that has only grown since, and I'm excited to see how this thinking develops as what it means to document a world forcibly opening itself in the name of capitalism reveals itself.

What does this chapbook DO (as much as it says or contains)?

It documents, it grieves, it mourns, it screams, it shakes its fist at the powers that be, and sometimes at the stars.

What would be the best possible outcome for this book? What might it do in the world and how will its presence as an object facilitate your creative role in your community and beyond? What are your hopes for this book, and for your practice?

The best outcome for this book would be for it to reach people who need it to remember, to get another perspective, to jog themselves out of the numbness and repressed memory that so many of us have struggled with lately... I would also love for it to constitute a kind of beginning for me and usher my work into the world as an emerging poet.

I'd be curious to hear some othings on the challenges we face in speking and publishing across lines of race, age, privilege, social/cultural background, and sexuality within the community, vs. the dangers of remaining and producing in isolated "silos."

This is a huge question and a huge conversation, always. I'll say this: I do not have an MFA and am coming into the poetic community as a queer disabled poet of color. I have found support and uplift from people who share those identities and people who do not because the New York poetry community is acutely aware of the need to diversify away from an exclusive focus on cis heteronormative white experience trained in form by higher institutions. It cannot be denied that institutional access allows for a smoother entry into the community and brings more visibility to one's work, but I have hope and perhaps some cruel optimism that when people come together in the name of our shared human right to create and share poetry, the work that speaks together will find some way to make it into the hands that need them.

Is there anything else we should have asked, or that you want to share?

I am in the process of working on a full collection of poetry that may include several of these poems and is also largely concerned with documentary poetics and what they can do and mean.

ABOUT THE AUTHOR

Author photo by Nicholas Tong

Ashna Ali is a queer agender Bangladeshi diasporic poet raised in Italy and based in Brooklyn. Their poems have appeared or are forthcoming in *Kajal Mag, Breadcrumbs Mag, Nat. Brut., The Felt, Bone Bouquet, HeART Online, No, Dear, Ginger Mag,* and *femmescapes*. They serve as Assistant Professor of Literature at Bard High School Early College Manhattan.

IG and Twitter: **@doctordushtu**
www.ashnaali.com

Image Description: Black and white headshot of Ashna Ali featuring their torso. They are turned slightly to the left and slightly smirking. They are wearing a sleeveless shirt with a high collar and have blonde highlights in their short hair. They are wearing a nose ring.

ABOUT THE AUTONOMOUS DOCUMENT INITIATIVE
and OS OPEN DESIGN PROTOCOL

This book was produced in 2020-21as a beta test version of the use of the OS Open Design Protocol resources and tools outside of the cohort model previously in operation.

While the OS publication initiative was designed around a horizontal, agile, decolonial open access vision (and has been able to remain aligned with these core principles in many ways) over the ten years of bringing in projects through a submission process and relying primarily on the labor of already precarious bodies / resources, it became abundantly clear that this was both unsustainable and limited in its capacities. Ultimately, the goal of these tools is to refuse the scarcity model, to dispel the illusion of merit, skill, or talent of a "few," and to invite all to the table for not only the making and growth inherent in creation and re/presentation both independently and in communty, but also to offer support in the documentation, archiving, and replication of work for present and future use and circulation.

With that in mind, I deduced that the way to truly scale the infrastructural offerings of the Operating System print/document concept was to translate the internal strategies and tools developed to support OS community members, facilitators, authors, artists, and collaborators from all disciplines into open access tools -- offering up blueprints to all not only for design thinking and editorial procedures, but also templates for organizational structure, agreements, and facilitated guidance for working outside of our comfort zone whether as writer, editor, designer, curator, or administrator. These, and so much more, can be found at the Open Resource Hub: https://www.theoperatingsystem.org/open-resource-library/

The goal is not the "success" of the documents made with The Operating System moniker, but a different success: one in which these tools support the continued seizing of the means of production by those who thought this impossible --the growth of DIY imprints, a ballooning refusal to pay into debt economies of submission and false legitimizing structures, the archiving, documentation, and distribution of vital ways of knowing and being, towards a future defined by autonomy and possibility. - Elæ Moss, 2021

WHY "PRINT/DOCUMENT"?

The Operating System uses the language "print/document" to differentiate from the book-object as part of our mission to distinguish the act of documentation-in-book-FORM from the act of publishing as a backwards-facing replication of the book's agentive *role* as it may have appeared the last several centuries of its history. Ultimately, I approach the book as TECHNOLOGY: one of a variety of printed documents (in this case, bound) that humans have invented and in turn used to archive and disseminate ideas, beliefs, stories, and other evidence of production.

Ownership and use of printing presses and access to (or restriction of printed materials) has long been a site of struggle, related in many ways to revolutionary activity and the fight for civil rights and free speech all over the world. While (in many countries) the contemporary quotidian landscape has indeed drastically shifted in its access to platforms for sharing information and in the widespread ability to "publish" digitally, even with extremely limited resources, the importance of publication on physical media has not diminished. In fact, this may be the most critical time in recent history for activist groups, artists, and others to insist upon learning, establishing, and encouraging personal and community documentation practices. Hear me out.

With The OS's print endeavors I wanted to open up a conversation about this: the ultimately radical, transgressive act of creating PRINT / DOCUMENTATION in the digital age. It's a question of the archive, and of history: who gets to tell the story, and what evidence of our life, our behaviors, our experiences are we leaving behind? We can know little to nothing about the future into which we're leaving an unprecedentedly digital document trail — but we can be assured that publications, government agencies, museums, schools, and other institutional powers that be will continue to leave BOTH a digital and print version of their production for the official record. Will we?

As a (rogue) anthropologist and long time academic, I can easily pull up many accounts about how lives, behaviors, experiences — how THE STORY of a time or place — was pieced together using the deep study of correspondence, notebooks, and other physical documents which are no longer the norm in many lives and practices. As we move our creative behaviors towards digital note taking, and even audio and video, what can we predict about future technology that is in any way assuring that our stories will be accurately told – or told at all? How will we leave these things for the record? In these documents we say:

> WE WERE HERE, WE EXISTED,
> WE HAVE A DIFFERENT STORY

- Elæ Moss, Founder/Creative Director, 2016

RECENT & FORTHCOMING
OS PRINT/DOCUMENTS AND PROJECTS, 2019-22

2020-22

UNLIMITED EDITIONS

Institution is a Verb: A Panoply Performance Lab Compilation - Esther Neff, Ayana Evans, Tsedaye Makonnen, Elizabeth Lamb, eds.
Daughter Isotope - Vidhu Aggarwal
Failure Biographies - Johnny Damm
Ginger Ko - Power ON
Danielle Pafunda - Spite
Robert Balun - Acid Western

KIN(D)* TEXTS AND PROJECTS

Intergalactic Travels: Poems from a Fugutive Alien - Alan Pelaez Lopez
HOAX - Joey De Jesus [Kin(d)*]
RoseSunWater - Angel Dominguez [Kin(d)*/Glossarium]
Bodies of Work - Elæ Moss & Georgia Elrod

GLOSSARIUM: UNSILENCED TEXTS AND TRANSLATIONS

Manhatitlán [Glossarium] - Steven Alvarez
Híkurí (Peyote) - José Vincente Anaya (tr. Joshua Pollock)
Vormorgen - Ersnt Toller tr. Mathilda Cullen [Glossarium x Kin(d)*; German-English]
Black and Blue Partition ('Mistry) - Monchoachi tr. Patricia Hartland [Glossarium; French & Antillean Creole/English]

IN CORPORE SANO

Hypermobilities - Ellen Samuels
Goodbye Wolf-Nik DeDominic

AUTONOMOUS DOCUMENT INITIATIVE

The Relativity of Living Well - Ashna Ali [In Corpore Sano x Kin(d)*]

2019
UNLIMITED EDITIONS

Ark Hive-Marthe Reed
I Made for You a New Machine and All it Does is Hope - Richard Lucyshyn
Illusory Borders-Heidi Reszies
A Year of Misreading the Wildcats - Orchid Tierney
Of Color: Poets' Ways of Making | An Anthology of Essays on Transformative Poetics - Amanda Galvan Huynh & Luisa A. Igloria, Editors

KIN(D)* TEXTS AND PROJECTS

A Bony Framework for the TangibleUniverse-- D. Allen [In Corpore Sano]
Opera on TV-James Brunton
Hall of Waters-Berry Grass
Transitional Object-Adrian Silbernagel

GLOSSARIUM: UNSILENCED TEXTS AND TRANSLATIONS

Śnienie / Dreaming - Marta Zelwan/Krystyna Sakowicz,
(Poland, trans. Victoria Miluch)
High Tide Of The Eyes - Bijan Elahi (Farsi-English/dual-language)
trans. Rebecca Ruth Gould and Kayvan Tahmasebian
In the Drying Shed of Souls: Poetry from Cuba's Generation Zero
Katherine Hedeen & Víctor Rodríguez Núñez, translators/editors
Street Gloss - Brent Armendinger w/ translations of
Alejandro Méndez, Mercedes Roffé, Fabián Casas,
Diana Bellessi & Néstor Perlongher (Argentina)
Operation on a Malignant Body - Sergio Loo
(Mexico, trans. Will Stockton)[In Corpore Sano]
Are There Copper Pipes in Heaven - Katrin Ottarsdóttir
(Faroe Islands, trans. Matthew Landrum)

DOCUMENT

/däkyəmənt/

First meant "instruction" or "evidence," whether written or not.

noun - a piece of written, printed, or electronic matter that provides information or evidence or that serves as an official record
verb - record (something) in written, photographic, or other form
synonyms - paper - deed - record - writing - act - instrument

[*Middle English, precept, from Old French, from Latin documentum, example, proof, from docre, to teach; see dek- in Indo-European roots.*]

Who is responsible for the manufacture of value?

Based on what supercilious ontology have we landed in a space where we vie against other creative people in vain pursuit of the fleeting credibilities of the scarcity economy, rather than freely collaborating and sharing openly with each other in ecstatic celebration of MAKING?

While we understand and acknowledge the economic pressures and fear-mongering that threatens to dominate and crush the creative impulse, we also believe that ***now more than ever we have the tools to redistribute agency via cooperative means,*** fueled by the fires of the Open Source Movement.

Looking out across the invisible vistas of that rhizomatic parallel country we can begin to see our community beyond constraints, in the place where intention meets resilient, proactive, collaborative organization.

Here is a document born of that belief, sown purely of imagination and will. When we document we assert. We print to make real, to reify our being there. When we do so with mindful intention to address our process, to open our work to others, to create beauty in words in space, to respect and acknowledge the strength of the page we now hold physical, a thing in our hand, we remind ourselves that, like Dorothy: *we had the power all along, my dears.*

the PRINT! DOCUMENT SERIES
is a project of
the trouble with bartleby
in collaboration with
the operating system

www.ingramcontent.com/pod-product-compliance
Lightning Source LLC
Chambersburg PA
CBHW030140100526
44592CB00011B/969